John MacKenzie

Condensed Temperance Facts for Christians

With remarks on ancient and modern wines and malt liquors

John MacKenzie

Condensed Temperance Facts for Christians
With remarks on ancient and modern wines and malt liquors

ISBN/EAN: 9783337329587

Printed in Europe, USA, Canada, Australia, Japan

Cover: Foto ©Lupo / pixelio.de

More available books at **www.hansebooks.com**

CONDENSED

TEMPERANCE FACTS

FOR CHRISTIANS.

WITH REMARKS ON

ANCIENT AND MODERN WINES

AND MALT LIQUORS.

— ✦ —

By J. MACKENZIE, M.D.,

JUSTICE OF THE PEACE, PROVOST OF INVERNESS, ETC.

"Buy the Truth, and sell it not."—SOLOMON.
"Have no fellowship with the unfruitful Works of Darkness, but rather reprove them."—ST PAUL.

LONDON:

TRÜBNER AND CO., 60, PATERNOSTER ROW.

1868.

PREFACE.

In the following Observations on Alcohol, I have to acknowledge being greatly indebted to my friend Dr F. R. Lees, in whose numerous works the history of intoxicants is investigated in a manner that creates astonishment at the immense amount of patient research bestowed on it by a truly philosophical and logical mind, such as is rarely indeed to be met with.

I have also profited by studying the Word of God, by the works of, or correspondence with, Baron Liebig, Mulder, Lyon Playfair, Christison, Carpenter, Day, Beaumont, Percy, Gairdiner, Johnston, Nott, and many other writers on the same subject in Britain, the Continent, and America; for without the light of chemistry and physiology to show the action of alcohol on the human body, abstainers can give no clear scientific reasons for refusing to drink intoxicating liquors. And without such proofs as these sciences afford, that alcohol is altogether and always injurious to health, however disguised under the names of wine, malt liquor, or cordials, it will be long ere Christians satisfy themselves that the drinking usages of society are *unchristian*, and dangerous to our hopes of eternal life.

I have written chiefly for *Christians*—lovers of God and man—under a conviction that ignorance as to the real action of alcohol on their health, mentally and bodily, is the sole reason why they hesitate to become abstainers; since all must admit the inconsistency of professing love to God and man, yet, at the same time, merely to gratify a lust, or to comply with a senseless custom, deliberately acting so as to injure that health of mind and body which we received from God expressly to glorify and serve Him on earth, and be of use to our fellow-creatures.

J. M.

I PROPOSE to show (1.) that alcohol in any form, whether pure or diluted, as in fermented wines and beer, is not food in any possible sense, but a mere poison; and that, even in moderation, it always injures the digestion, the blood, brain, and nervous system, and must impair health and shorten life. *Its use must, therefore, be anti-Christian.*

2. That *fermented* grape juice, called 'wine,' contains nothing deserving the name of 'food,' or worthy the title 'generous,' but consists merely of plain water, alcohol, and some minute microscopic atoms, useless either as food or medicine; and that its sole active principle, for good or for evil, is alcohol.

3. That there are *two* kinds of wine made from grape juice—the one, unfermented, containing the nourishment found in the grape; the other, fermented, having its nourishment destroyed by fermentation, and its sugar converted into the poison called alcohol. And that all fermented wines are alike void of nourishment, differing from each other only in their amount of water, alcohol,

colouring matter, and flavour ; except sparkling wines, which, like soda water, contain a little carbonic acid gas.

4. That malt liquors also called beer, of various qualities, simply differ from each other in their proportions of water, alcohol, colouring matter, and flavour, when fully fermented, contain no flesh-forming principle ; and when, as ordinarily met with, *not* fully fermented till emptied into their votaries' unhappy stomachs, contain *so* little nourishment, that of about 450lbs. of barley required to make 730 quarts of ordinary beer, all but 20 ounces of flesh-forming matter in the 450lbs. has been utterly destroyed in forming the alcohol—on account of which alone the beer is valued and drank. With these undeniable facts before us, there cannot be a doubt that the prescribing of fermented wines or malt liquor as nourishing food, or prescribing one variety as more nourishing than another, is a proof of gross ignorance in the sciences of chemistry, of physiology, and of histology—the science of the formation of the human body.

Temperance Facts for Christians.

―――◄••►―――

RDENT SPIRIT, or a liquid that will take fire and burn away, is obtained by distillation from sugary liquids fermented. Separate from such liquids, it was unknown till the 13th century, when some Arabian 'alchemists,' searching for the 'Philosopher's Stone'—which they imagined had the power of converting everything it touched into gold—discovered this deadly poison, for which, unlike other poisons, no antidote has been found.

Had the 'alchemists' been in search of the 'Policeman's Stone'—as we may well term alcohol, since it is able to petrify the human heart as we daily and hourly see in our criminal courts and prisons—they might well have been congratulated by Satan on their discovery ; for, since the fall of man, assuredly nothing has been discovered so capable of opening the doors of hell, and preventing its votaries from loving God and striving to enter in at the straight gate that leads to 'eternal life,' as alcohol. Its discoverer probably had some personal experience of its mischievous properties, since he well named it, in Arabic, 'Al-Ghoul' (the evil spirit), whence its modern name of al-cohol.

When distilled from fermented wine, it is known by the name of brandy ; from cane sugar, rum ; from malt sugar, whisky; and these and all other varieties of alcohol *merely differ from each other in flavour*. All are 'intoxicants,' that is, ' poisons,' possessing generally the same irritant, astringent, and sedative properties. The *irritant* nature of alcohol will at once be felt if dropped into an eye or wound : or, if we hold some in the mouth for five minutes, inflammation of the inside of the cheeks will be both *seen* and *felt*, even by its greatest previous admirer. And the same effect occurs when alcohol is drank ; although, owing to our gullet and stomach being out of sight, we only *feel* the burning heat of the inflammation which it excites.

Retained in the mouth for a longer time, the irritation and inflammation pass into blisters ; and we may then observe its *sedative* powers, the nerves of taste becoming so completely paralysed that they cannot distinguish the taste of one substance from another. Yet, by perseverance in the use of alcohol, the unwise come to enjoy this burning inflammatory sensation, regardless of its ultimate serious effect on their health. The *sedative* (that is, 'putting to rest') power of alcohol is also, when drank, too often visible in the confusion of mind which it causes in the brain, passing into paralysis of the nerves which direct our muscular movements ; so that the poisoned person often becomes unable to stand or walk. And when the dose is large—especially if taken on an empty stomach—alcohol is a more deadly sedative than even prussic acid.

As an *astringent*, alcohol hardens and tans all vegetable or animal substances, so that, in contact with it, they become imperishable. This effect on various things immersed in alcohol (in glass jars or bottles) may be seen on our museum shelves.

The experiments of MM. Lallemand, Perrin, and Duroy, of Paris ; Dr E. Smith, of London, and others, show that alcohol (which contains nothing *capable* of assimilation into the vital structure of our bodies) is always expelled as alcohol by the lungs, kidneys, skin, etc., unaltered in any way—thus differing entirely from substances which are digested, altered, and assimilated, and then become homogeneous with our flesh, bone, and blood ;—proving clearly that alcohol *cannot*, in any sense, be termed food or nourishment.

My friend Professor Christison, apparently averse to condemn an agreeable old acquaintance as a mere poison, writes of it thus :—" I suspect alcohol will be found to belong to the new tribe of agents—' paratriptics' let us call them—not altogether bad, although not nutrients." This term means ' waste-lessener,' and has been invented by physiologists who imagine that various substances have the power to prevent the natural periodical wasting away, or moulting, of those parts of our bodies which have served their time, and whose place is to be re-occupied by fresh food eaten, digested, and carried into the blood for this end alone.

But it will be obvious, even to the unlearned, that any substance which can arrest the natural process of decay and renewal, so wonderfully planned by our Maker, must be neither more nor less than a mischievous poison most adverse to health ; for the retention in our bodies of that which nature strives to cast out, necessarily involves such a disturbance of the normal, easy, healthy operations going on, as can only be rightly termed '*dis-ease.*' According as the retention of the used-up parts is for a short time, and to a trifling extent, or the contrary, the disturbance and disease will be slight or serious : but it is evident that any substance which *disturbs* our bodies, and thus causes disease, should be considered as a 'poison'; and this term, abstainers are satisfied, is a more simple and better name for alcohol than its new name of ' paratriptic.'

Alcohol acts powerfully on the gastric juice.   This liquid is secreted by the inner coat of the stomach for the purpose of digesting (*i.e.* dissolving) certain vegetable and all animal substances with which it comes in contact ; for the food we eat to support life would be of no more use to us than a stone, were it not melted down to a gruel, in order to its being absorbed (*i.e.* drank up) by vessels whose mouths open for that purpose all over the inner coat of the intestines. In fact, the stomach is merely the kitchen where, in health, our food is prepared for passing into the bowels, in order that the absorbent vessels may there seize upon all its nourishing matter when passing by. The useless parts are left to continue on in their course until ejected from the body.

The nourishment thus absorbed into the blood goes to every part of our bodies where it is needed ; for, though not visibly to our dull senses, our bodies are continually decaying and being renewed—hence new, healthy matter is required to take the place of those parts which have served their time and then decay. Therefore, whatever injures the digestion of our food, or retards its being taken up and carried where it is required, injures our health, *and must, of course, tend to shorten life.* Supposing the used-up parts of our bodies continuing to be thrown off, while no sufficient supply óf nourishment is passed along the bowels for the absorbent vessels to take up, and thus supply the waste going on, we should then 'starve to death.' This fatal result sometimes does occur, in consequence of disease in these vessels rendering them unable to absorb the required nourishment.

Hence the necessity of having (1st) a supply of nourishing digestible food in the stomach, and (2nd) a supply of healthy rennet to dissolve this food and prepare it for being taken up and passed into the blood. Indeed, without healthy rennet in our stomachs, we should starve to death, even if all the food in the world were at our command. And thus we see clearly how anything that injures the supply, or the dissolving powers of our rennet, is a *mischievous poison.* The amount of injury may be small or great, according to the dose or the constitution ; but *a Christian* will not measure such injury by its extent, but will shrink from what can in any way or degree injure his health. 'Gratifying a vitiated taste,' or 'complying with the (senseless) drinking usages of society,' is no fit excuse to offer to God at the great day of account for diminished powers of usefulness and shortened life.

The rennet contains a digestive principle called *pepsine,* which is now prepared from the rennet of calves', dogs', and pigs' stomachs ; and is frequently prescribed as a remedy for indigestion, from a belief that it may assist the patients' own weak or unhealthy rennet.

No rennet is found in the healthy stomach till its coat is excited by food, when it is plentifully poured out, ready to act on any digestible matter. (*See* BEAUMONT on 'DIGESTION,' p. 96, etc.)

As soon as alcohol enters our stomachs, it comes in contact with this transparent fluid, and instantly the ' pepsine ' is ' precipitated ' (in chemical language) —*i.e.* separates from it—in the form of a grey coloured sediment, and digestion ceases till a fresh supply of rennet is provided.   The alcohol next proceeds to condense, astringe, or tan the food, the digestion of which had ceased by the alcoholic precipitation of the pepsine in the first supply of rennet, and a fresh supply of rennet is demanded in order to 'try its hand' on the food which the alcohol has rendered more tough and indigestible.

These undeniable *facts*, admitted now by every physiologist, explain clearly why persons who drink alcohol when fasting, are much more easily affected by it than when it finds rennet and food in the stomach.   In the *empty* stomach, 'the evil spirit' finds no occupation, and proceeds at once on its main errand of mischief to the blood and brain ; while in the *full* stomach, it is for a time busily occupied—first in precipitating the pepsine, and then in tanning the food.

Having done its work in the stomach, the alcohol is absorbed by numberless vessels opening into the stomach, and thus gets into the blood, which carries it to the brain, so that, through the nerves, it may act upon all the mental and muscular organs of our bodies, till expelled by means of the lungs, skin, kidneys, etc.

It is by means of the blood that alcohol finds its way to every part of our bodies within a minute or two after it has been drank, as can easily be proved by smelling the patient's breath, however well the mouth has been washed out.   Mothers, who would be shocked at hearing of nurse having given baby 'a dram' at the gin shop

should know that, as soon as nurse has had her prescribed daily allowance of wine, malt liquor, or punch,
' to strengthen her,' there will be no difficulty whatever
in *distilling spirit from the milk !*

Our blood is composed of water, and innumerable
miscroscopic red globules floating in it.   Physiologists
agree with Moses in believing (Lev. xvii. 2) that 'the
life of the flesh is in the blood'; and are now satisfied
that the digested and absorbed food is carried to nourish
every part of our bodies by means of these red globules.
In experimenting with alcohol, to ascertain its action on
the blood, Schultz, Munroe, and others, found that when
alcohol and its red globules meet, the latter contract to
a point, and then disappear—their colouring matter
passes into the general stream of the blood, which is
thus rendered less able to absorb oxygen, and give off
the carbonic acid found in the venous blood ready to be
thrown out of the body, in order to its again becoming
pure and healthy, and of a bright crimson colour, but
which thus remains dark coloured, and unable to carry
on its appointed work.

The colouring matter of the destroyed globules
escaping, and being forced into the fine hair-like ends of
the blood vessels, causes irritation and various local
diseases ; and many physiologists believe that such injury
to the circulation, in the delicate glands of the lungs,
is the exciting cause of consumption.

The natural amount of fat in healthy blood is from 2
to 3 parts in 100; but in the blood of drunkards, the
eminent chemist Le Canu found nearly 12 parts in 100!
This accumulated fat is deposited very frequently where
t is most injurious to health—as, for instance, in the
muscles of the heart—often causing death in those who

drink freely of intoxicating liquors, though never found thus fatally misplaced in abstainers.

Nothing is more common than to hear alcohol praised as ‘food,’ *because* its votaries sometimes grow fat. But the deposit of fat is simply a provision of God to aid in purifying the blood—its fat being thus stored away till it can by got rid of by exercise, without which it would soon occasion not only great discomfort, but even destroy life. Indeed, a farmer who tried to fatten an animal which had daily hard exercise, would be considered insane.

Those who are accustomed to use the microscope, can frequently tell, by examining a drop of blood from a person in seeming health, whether it belonged to an abstainer or to a drinker of alcohol ;—the globules in the abstainer’s blood being healthy, while many of those in the blood even of moderate drinkers are visibly altered.

Professor Dieffenbach, of Berlin, says he can tell at once when the body of an abstainer is under his surgical knife, the muscles offering great resistance, and being firm and high coloured when divided ; while those of the intemperate are flabby and of a pale colour. Thus a drunkard’s wound heals with difficulty ; and when the powerful, fat, handsome-looking London brewers’ draymen meet even with a trifling accident, it generally proves fatal. These men can hardly be termed drunkards, yet their blood has become diseased by beer drinking, although the strongest beer contains only about one-eighth part of alcohol.

All our secretions—such as bile, saliva, rennet, etc.—are formed from our blood. Alcohol disturbs the circulation, and *cannot* be drank without *some* of the blood globules (its vital principle) being injured. Hence it is *quite impossible* that blood so disturbed and damaged can (all other things being equal) secrete such a supply of healthy rennet as the blood of a person not thus injured by alcohol.

Those who study Beaumont, on 'Digestion' (pp. 248–254), will never trust to their sensations in preference to their reason in regard to the action of alcohol on the body; for at the very moment when St. Martin (with the exception of a little headache and foul tongue) declared he was, and seemed to be, in ordinary health— nay, even said he was hungry—Dr Beaumont's eye saw the coats of his stomach (perfectly healthy before his intoxication) actually inflamed, ulcerated, and even bleeding, in consequence of the action of alcohol upon them !

Persons thus injured are often foolishly advised to drink *more* alcohol, and are deceived, by its temporary sedative action, into thinking it does them good ; while, in truth, it has been protracting the disease, and merely silencing some of its painful *sensations*, the monitors of mischief going on.

The dram-drinker, after his glass of liquor, feels an agreeable, warm, inward glow ; and the cause of this not being visible, or explained to him, he believes the dram has done him good. But could he (like Dr Beaumont) *see* that this pleasant warm sensation was caused by inflammation in the gullet and stomach, and observe that it was followed by injured digestion, damaged blood, and even ulceration of the stomach, diseased liver and kidneys, his visits to the dram shop would, unless he were positively insane, become 'few and far between.'

Dr Beaumont states that these appearances and effects in the stomach were not merely observed occasionally, but *invariably*, when St. Martin had been drinking to what is termed ' excess.'

Our senses frequently are injured, and need aid from science, as in the case of the eye dim from age, deafness, etc. Experience tells us that drops of pure water falling on a polished marble slab will in time bore a hole into or through it, as surely as a mason's iron could do ; and although our dim senses do not see a visible impression made by the first drop of water, the wise will hesitate to say that none has been made till they have examined matters by the aid of science. So, *we* may not *see* any permanent injury to our health by taking a dram, any more than we see a depression made in the marble slab by the first drop of water ; but it is as positively certain that the dram *has* made an injurious impression on the health of the person who drank it, as that the drop of water has done so on the solid stone or marble.

Till within a few years, medical men bled their patients for almost every disease. Physiology now clearly shows that bleeding merely weakens our system ; and, where it does not *kill*, delays recovery. Bleeding, therefore, is now abandoned by all well-educated persons.

Physiology—even more strongly than in the case of bleeding—now shows that alcohol is nothing but a poison, always detrimental to animal health. But this declaration is more unpalatable than its protest against bleeding ; for alcohol is generally allowed both by physician and patient, and can only be given up at some sacrifice to the palate, to which may frequently be added the risk of ridicule and the contempt of fools. A medical man or a clergyman, who drinks and loves alcohol, whether in the form of spirit, or beer, or wine, or uses tobacco, even in moderation, cannot well tell others that these things are mischievous, and yet hope to be respected as morally and intellectually wise.

The celebrated Dr Gregory used to say that ' he never got a patient from water drinking, but thousands from drinking alcohol '; and as ill-disposed persons hint that this is a reason why many medical men hesitate to recommend abstinence, the wise should escape from so degrading a suspicion as to their motives.

Thousands of medical men have now publicly declared alcohol to be a mere poison, but the majority are still unwilling to give up what they and their patients so dearly love, and so recommend moderation in the use of what they ought to *know* is injurious.   Many, probably for want of time, have not studied the subject as it deserves.   They commenced practice before chemistry and physiology had shown the true action of alcohol on the body, and constant professional labour has too often allowed no sufficient opportunities of searching into this and many other matters of importance.   As in the case of bleeding, public opinion will grow so strong that they will be compelled to inquire, and at last swim with the tide. Till then, nothing is more natural than that people should shut their eyes and ears to an unpalatable truth, and lay the blame of this folly on the shoulders of their doctors, who at least *ought* to know ' what is truth,' and act up to what is now so clearly established.

Since, therefore, alcohol injures the digestion and devitalizes the blood, it follows that (other circumstances being equal) no alcohol drinker can possibly enjoy such good health, or live so long, as an abstainer, as is **distinctly proved by examining Life Assurance tables.**

B

In the United Kingdom Temperance Provident
Mutual Assurance Office, while all parties pay the same
premium, a note of those paid by abstainers is kept
separate from those paid by the moderate drinkers (no
Assurance society admitting the intemperate), and at the
end of five years—as in other mutual Assurance offices—
the whole profits are divided: the profit in the abstainers'
section among the abstainers, and those of the moderate
drinkers among that class of subscribers. And taking a
group of offices, we find the average mortality has been
17 per 1,000, while in the same period only 7½ per
1,000 died in the abstainers' section of the Temperance
Provident Institution—thus proving beyond all dispute
that even the moderate use of alcohol shortens life.
And when we remember the care which assurance office
directors take in the selection of good lives among their
constituents, and also that probably most of the abstainers in these offices had at one period of their lives injured their health by the use of alcohol, even a brewer,
or a distiller, or a wine merchant, might be convinced
from these *facts* that their trades may well be termed,
' death in the pot.'

Alcohol acts more fatally in hot than in temperate
climates. In six months of the year 1838, we find it
stated in the Friend of India of Oct. 24, 1839, that 10.
20 per cent. of alcohol drinking British soldiers entered
the hospitals, while only 2.65 per cent. of abstainers did
so ; and from the Statistical Society's Journal (May,
1857) we find that in the Madras army, only 11 per 1000
abstaining soldiers died, for every 23 per 1000 of their
moderate drinking, and 44 per 1000 of their intemperate
comrades. But on this subject there seems now to be
only one opinion; although those in power still shame-

fully hesitate to take the necessary steps for saving our soldiers' lives. God evidently intended man to live for at least 70 or 80 years, although from carelessness and ignorance, or the faults of our ancestors, comparatively few attain to that age.

We are frequently asked to observe, that A or B, who has notoriously 'taken his liquor like a man,' lived to a good old age, as proving that alcohol does not injure health! But inquiry will satisfy the impartial, that few indeed of the hard drinkers live long, and we must remember that it is not fair to take single lives in a matter like this, but that the truth is only to be found by taking the average of large numbers of persons, as in Assurance office returns.

For instance, many paupers live to a great age, who from childhood have never been *lodged*, *clothed*, or *fed*, as every physiologist admits that persons require to be, if they expect to enjoy health ; these three things being the main points towards longevity.

Now it would be quite as unreasonable to argue from such aged paupers, that good lodging, clothing, and feeding were of no value as regards health, as it is to assert, from the occasional aged intemperate person, that alcohol is not poison.

Most poisons select a particular part of our bodies on which they directly act. We find arsenic affecting the lining coats of the stomach and bowels, strychnia acting on the spinal marrow and the nerves proceeding from it ; opium on the heart and brain ; while alcohol, distinguished by its powerful action on the brain, is well termed a 'brain poison.'

A very small dose immediately impairs the natural clearness of mind which every person desires, whenever he is placed in a situation involving personal danger. The moderate drunkard, if I may use such a term, may have full power to use the muscles of his arm or leg, yet have his brain so poisoned by the alcohol, that when it should direct the foot to step straight out, it as often tells it to step sideways, and its foolish owner has thus frequent cause to complain more of the breadth than of the length of the road between the public house and his own home.

The rapidity with which alcohol passes from the stomach to the brain, may be learned from an experiment of Dr Percy, in which having passed about half an ounce of it into a dog's stomach, its heart ceased to beat in two minutes, and the dog being instantly killed, alcohol was distilled from its brain, proving that it must have passed from the stomach into the blood, and thence into the brain, within the two minutes when the heart ceased to beat and to circulate the blood! It has been found so abundantly in the cavities of the brain after a fatal debauch, that it has burnt with a blue flame when taken up with a teaspoon, and thrown into the fire.

It acts chiefly on those parts of the brain which are the seat of the lower or animal passions, and when much excited, these lower parts seem to obscure all the more noble principles that distinguish man from beasts that perish. Hence the vast majority of crimes based upon 'envy, malice, and all uncharitableness,' are caused by the brain poison alcohol *stirring up all the worst elements of our nature*, and weakening or destroying all good principles. Nothing is more common than for a drunken person to commit murder in the most cruel and determined manner, who, when sober, was noted for a kind, amiable disposition, and who on restoration to his senses, had merely a confused remembrance of some trifling quarrel. Surely then, Christians seeing such frightful consequences from the brain poison, should avoid it in every form as they would avoid Satan, lest it destroy *their* senses also, and lead them to shame and sorrow. They should not only pray that *God* may not lead them into temptation, but should do *all they can* to avoid the temptation.

It is also quite certain that the drunkard's brain, by ill-usage, loses the power of distinguishing between what is good and right, and what is evil and wrong. Even in matters of ordinary business (other circumstances being equal), an alcohol drinker is no match for an abstainer.

How well gamblers understand this fact may be seen in their dens of crime, where 'alcohol, in its most tempting forms, is at command of their votaries (often gratis), while the keepers of these dens never taste one drop till the games are ended! No such mischief to the brain results from other poisons. We never hear of persons *murdering* their neighbours from having taken an over dose of arsenic, strychnia, or opuim, etc. Those who argue that Christians, when they eat too much beef or bread, or drink too much water, are as blameworthy as persons who drink too much alcohol, *forget* that such excess in things necessary to support life, merely injures the individuals themselves, while the alcohol drinker injures not only himself, but, in numberless ways, his neighbour also. Besides, God will not excuse *our* faults because others also do what is wrong. Everyone has to answer for himself.

It is a subject of constant national shame that the government and magistracy professing to be Christian, which sees and admits that alcohol is the cause of most of our national crime and misery, should in every way support and encourage its use, instead of viewing its manufacture and sale as a dreadful crime. May God send down the spirit of light and love, and then alcohol will be treated as it deserves, and as it is well named, *Satan's Chloroform.*

An Australian newspaper lately mentioned that the leader of a flock of sheep there, having jumped into a dry watercourse from which there was no exit, the whole flock, in spite of the attending shepherd's greatest exertions, followed him, and became so heaped up over each other, that many of them were suffocated.

We can imagine the alcohol drinker exclaiming, 'Well, to be sure, what stupid brutes sheep are!' Indeed? Some people think that man is not less stupid, nay even less excusable, when, warned to avoid a pit in which some 50,000 or more of his comrades are yearly smothered in Britain alone, he carelessly or angrily refuses to listen to the friendly warning, 'Take care.'

As an example of the power of alcohol to harden the heart and destroy every kindly feeling, rendering even seeming Christians utterly indifferent to the fate of crowds who are murdered by alcohol all around them, I was reading lately to a lady (who is apparently as mindful of her duties towards her children and the poor and helpless, as any of her neighbours) that, during the year 1865, 145 inquests had been held in Liverpool alone, on infants 'overlaid' or smothered by their mothers, *chiefly on Saturday and Sunday nights*; and expressing my horror at such a frightful list of palpable *spirit murders* in a Christian land—her only observation was, 'They must have a jolly time of it there on Saturday nights!'

I need hardly add, this lady hates the very word 'abstain.'

A wonderful delusion prevails as to the real composition and value of ordinary wine. Supposing it to be made from grape juice (although it is very often made from cider, etc.), people imagine that as grapes are a nourishing food, ordinary wine must *therefore* be nourishing! On this most erroneous idea medical men prescribe, and patients drink, what they call 'generous' wine, as 'a most valuable tonic,' praising it as the actual 'staff of life,' or at least as a sheet anchor in disease.

Now, when grape juice is fermented, its albumen and sugar, the only useful substances worthy of notice found in grapes, are converted into yeast and alcohol, for which last only wine is drank. Few grapes contain sufficient sugar to render the wine made from them as intoxicating as is desired, so an additional dose of alcohol is added, and this is called fortifying the wine.

100 parts of ordinary sherry as sold in Britain consists of about 76 parts plain water; 23 parts alcohol; and the remaining one part is composed of above 50 different microscopic atoms, all of which, except the atom of sugar not fermented away, are equally useless either as food or medicine.

The proverb that 'Doctors differ,' is in nothing more conspicuous than in their prescriptions of wine, and other intoxicants.

One warns his patients only to drink the compound named 'Port.' The next declares that 'Claret' alone is the elixir of life, and 'Port' mere poison. A third recommends old Madeira. A fourth 'Sherry.' And I remember once accompanying a late dying monarch's physician in London searching for 'old Malaga', as the only wine suited to the Royal malady

Now, although it may surprise many of my readers, it is nevertheless a simple, undeniable chemical fact, that, except in colour, amount of alcohol, and difference in flavour, all *genuine wines are in composition all but precisely alike*, not one of them possessing a single atom more valuable than another, either as food or medicine!

So that those who prescribe fermented wine, as nourishing or tonic, and at the same time tell us that plain spirits are *not* nourishing or tonic, are either wilfully imposing on their friends, or else are grossly ignorant of chemistry and physiology. [*See page* 36.]

Many persons declaim against spirit dealers and spirit drinkers, and will not allow any kind of 'plain spirits' to enter their houses—'rank poison,' as they justly call them. Yet, absurd as it may appear, these well meaning but ignorant persons purchase, and drink, and give to their friends, this *identical rank poison*, only concealed under the colour, flavour, price, and more fashionable name of *wine!*

These are hard, positive facts, which no man alive pretending to know even the rudiments of chemistry and physiology now ventures to deny, and the only excuse for such ignorance and folly, is persons believing that medical men *must* know the truth in regard to intoxicating liquors, and the uncharitableness of thinking that, knowing the truth, they conceal it from their patients.

But most young students of medicine attend to the study of chemistry only so far as is absolutely necessary to enable them to get through their examinations, generally passing at once from college to a life of laborious practice, and never finding time for returning to study chemistry, which most of them consider as one of the mere accomplishments of the profession.

Then again, physicians can only *guess* at their patients' internal ailments, and are very often deceived by the visible symptoms, prescribing remedies that, owing to mistaking the disease, too often hurry their patients to the grave.

Not long ago medical men pointed to many recoveries after vigorous bleeding, as a proof of its being a wise remedy; just as they now point to typhus patients, saved, as *they* think, by the use of wine or spirits; and quite forget, *amidst the crowds who die of the remedy*, that some recover *in spite of* such most irrational, and now well proved murderous, treatment.

Those who have not studied ancient history believe there never was, nor can be, any sort of 'wine' but fermented and alcoholic. Let such as desire to know the truth turn to Homer's Odyssey, written 884 years before Christ, and they will there find that the famous Maronean 'wine' required 20 waters ere it could be drank! When grape juice is fermented, its sugar, which alone renders it thick and syrupy, is converted into thin, watery-like alcohol; and Ulysses must have been all but an abstainer before he would have added 20 waters to the most alcoholic modern wine ever heard of—nay, even to pure alcohol itself.

There cannot be a doubt that the Maronean wine was *grape juice boiled down* till nothing but a treacle-like *syrup* remained, and which would keep for a long time.

If it be suggested that Homer's wine must have been fermented and alcoholic, else how came it about that

> 'themselves they lost,
> And drank oblivion of their native coast,'—

we reply in Homer's own words,

'mix'd was the bowl,
With *drug of power* to quench the soul'—

evidently the same intoxicating '*mixed wine*' so frequently mentioned in Scripture, and by ancient writers,
as ruinous both to soul and body.

Aristotle, 384 B.C. (Meteor: iv. 10), says, 'The stronger
Arcadian wines were reduced to a concrete mass by
heat.' This, of course, *must* have been done *before* the
grape sugar was converted by fermentation into alcohol,
for it would puzzle the most clever cook or chemist to
reduce a bottle of any fermented alcoholic wine to a
concrete mass. It would evaporate, under heat, into
a few pinches of snuff!

Aristotle's term 'stronger,' here clearly means 'more
firm,' the amount of sugar in grape juice varying much,
according to soil, climate, etc. Grapes grown in warm
climates generally contain more sugar than those in colder
regions ; and the more sugar in the grape the 'stronger'
the 'wine,' whether as syrup or as fermented into alcohol.

Writing of the Arcadian wines, Aristotle says, 'They
were dried in skins, in order to their being drank when
grated down.' Meaning, of course, when grated or
scraped down into water, just as *fruit jellies* are now
frequently dissolved in water as a cooling drink.

Again (lib. iv.) he says, 'Only one canton of all
Lycaonia produced wines not condensed by smoke or
fire. All elsewhere were reduced to a paste, and cut
with a knife.' Yet those who don't or won't inquire,
insist that *all* ancient wine, even though 'condensed,'
was exactly the same as our modern fermented alcoholic
poison; and because 'wine' is spoken of in the Bible as
sometimes a good thing, they insist that *therefore* modern
alcoholic wine must be good also !

When we thus know, from Aristotle and others, that whole districts of country carefully preserved their grape juice from fermentation in ancient times, it is quite as reasonable for abstainers to infer from this that fermented wine was then unknown, as for non-abstainers to insist, as they do, that all wine in these early times, and when our Saviour lived on earth, was fermented and alcoholic.

Aristophanes (429 B.C.) says, 'The Pramnian wine shrivelled the features and obstructed the bowels; while to drink the Corinthian was absolute torture!' These wines were clearly not simply grape juice, whether fermented or unfermented, but wine 'mixed' with drugs to suit a vitiated palate.

Cato (232 B.C.), says, 'The Coan wine was exposed to the sun for thirty or forty days in summer, for four years, and at night returned to the more moderate heat of the Apotheca; it was then *firm* and *knotty*;'—the exact description of grape sugar as found in old dry raisins.

Virgil (70 B.C.—Georgic iii.) writes of 'cleaving the coagulated wine with hatchets,' on the northern shore of the Black Sea,—the syrup evidently having become candied from cold.

In Georgic ii. 97, he writes of 'vina firmissima,' (most solid wines), just as a modern wine merchant praises his 'full-bodied' compounds.

Ovid (43 B.C.) in his Tristia, i. 3, says, the Bulgarians used their wine in lumps. 'Nec hausta mea, sed data frustra bibunt.' *Cakes of wine.*

Pliny (A.D. 23), and many others, write of wine only drinkable when dissolved in hot water. Such wine never *could* have borne any essential resemblance to our modern alcoholic liquor. And he writes further of the celebrated

Opimian wine (which was made v.c. 633), as being then
150 years old; and, with Martial, says it was *like honey*,
and when used was mixed with water. He says, grape
juice was boiled down in leaden cauldrons, iron or
bronze injuring the flavour. Plutarch, Columella, Palla-
dius, Athenadorus, Varro, Tibullus, Athenæus, Andreas
Baccius, and others, all write of 'WINE' as 'thick,'
'firm,' 'knotty,' 'solid,' 'syrupy,' or 'sugary,' and of its
being dissolved in water when drank.

Galen, the celebrated ancient physician, who lived
A. D. 131 (Meth. Med. xii. 4), mentions the Aminean
wines as 'vina firmissima' (most solid); undoubtedly
boiled-down grape syrup.

St Basil (A.D. 328), writing to Cesarius, says, 'The
hermits brought the consecrated bread into the desert
with them for a year's supply, but could not preserve the
wine so long.' Had it been fermented alcoholic wine,
they could have had no difficulty whatever in this respect,
but the only wine known to them, evidently, was simple
grape juice, which, unless carefully prepared by evapora-
tion, is very apt to ferment, and as *they* supposed, was
then unfit for use. Indeed, in early times water was
always mixed with the communion 'wine,' doubtless
because the grape syrup was too thick to be drank con-
veniently undiluted. We learn from the Evangelists, that
what our Lord used at the Last Supper was not our
modern wine, but the 'fruit of the vine,'—most probably the fresh-expressed grape juice, such as Pharaoh's
butler was in the habit of preparing for his master's use.
(See Genesis, xl. 11). Indeed, we may be quite certain
that *unfermented* grape juice was used at the last supper,
because the Jews most carefully removed not merely
leavened bread, but *every fermented article* out of their

houses at the Passover. Even now, the Jews are equally careful, and in order to make sure that their Passover wine is not fermented, frequently make it for the occasion from a decoction of raisins. No unprejudiced person can read these testimonies and still insist that all ancient wine was like our modern, fermented, intoxicating liquors.

Abstainers do not assert that no fermented alcoholic wine was ever met with of old. All they insist on is, that while there *may* have been alcoholic (as there undoubtedly was mixed and drugged) wine ; unfermented, boiled down, nourishing grape juice was often made and used under the name of ' wine ' ; nay, as in the case of the Opimian, was looked upon as 'the best wine.' It is also quite certain that such grape syrup was, as described by Pliny and others, often mixed with drugs, many of which might intoxicate, or stupify and make drunken, although the wine did not and could not contain much alcohol, if any.

Abstainers assert, however, that our Saviour could not have given *fermented* grape juice, or any alcoholic liquor, to His disciples at the last supper, without utterly disregarding the positive commands given in Exodus xii. 15, regarding the forms to be observed at the Passover. ' Ye shall put away leaven (*i.e.* ferment) out of your houses.'

Now, when we know to a certainty that harmless, nourishing, unintoxicating grape juice was constantly in use at feasts, etc., both before and after our Saviour's time, surely it is only natural and reasonable to believe that the Son of God converted the water into similar '*good wine*,' in His miracle at Cana. It is in truth nothing short of blasphemy, to say that Jesus, who through the Spirit everywhere warns us to beware of intoxicating wine as soul-destroying, deliberately made and gave about 100 gallons of this soul-destroying liquor to people who had already well drank of it.

Had He acted in such direct opposition to His doctrine and character, He never could have ventured to ask His enemies, 'Which of you convinceth me of sin?' for the rudest and most thoughtless even of the Gentiles would instantly have referred to his alleged conduct at Cana as utterly shameful and sinful.

The same delusion which exists everywhere on the subject of fermented alcoholic wine, prevails generally regarding the fermented liquors made from malt, and known by the name of BEER.

Because barley contains much nourishing food, those who are unacquainted with chemistry imagine that the nourishment remains in the malt liquor made from it! This is as complete a mistake as the popular error regarding fermented grape juice.

Baron Liebig, in his Letters on Chemistry, 1844, p. 57, says, 'Beer, wine, spirits, etc., furnish no elements capable of entering into the composition of blood, muscular fibre, or any part which is the seat of the vital principle.' Again, ' 730 gallons of the best Bavarian beer contain exactly as much nourishment as a 5 lbs. loaf, or 3 lbs. of beef.' No one has yet ventured to dispute this statement. It took at least 1,200 lbs. of barley food, converted into malt, to make these 730 gallons of beer; the fermentation, however, destroyed the whole of this food excepting 5 lbs; the end being that the beer drinker might gratify a vitiated palate at the expense of injuring his stomach, liver, brain, and blood, by the alcohol formed in the process of fermentation! Can conduct like this be termed rational or Christ-like?

Our Lord changed innocent water into natural, nourishing wine ; but the brewer changes solid nourishment into liquid poison.

Professor Lyon Playfair says, ' 100 parts of ordinary beer or porter contain 9·5 parts of solid matter ; of which only 0·6 parts consist of flesh-forming matters ; or, in other words, it takes 1,666 parts of ordinary beer or porter to obtain one part of nourishing matter.' He adds, ' Beer is not taken as a beverage for its nutritious ingredients, but *wholly* for its alcohol.'

With these undenied and undeniable facts open to the world's inquiry, established by those who excel all others in the science of chemistry, and who certainly have no abstaining bias, surely we are fully justified in calling on Christians to consider this matter seriously.

We frequently offer up public prayers to God for favourable weather, in order that our farmers may prepare the soil for seed, or that the grain may ripen and be safely gathered, so as to supply food for man and beast ; yet every year we see more and more of this very grain converted into malt (and by Sabbath labour), and then, all but as completely and utterly destroyed in our distilleries and breweries as if it were burnt to ashes !—nay, far worse than this, converted into the poisonous alcohol, which is notoriously the chief cause of the crime, poverty, shame, and misery of our land.

Scotland produces yearly about five million quarters of grain ; and above eight million quarters of grain are yearly destroyed in Britain by conversion into beer or spirits !

It is indeed worse than national insanity, when, with science declaring to all who choose to inquire, that this is a wholesale and wanton destruction of our food, yea after year passes by, and no change for the better is thought of or cared for, except by abstainers, who are talked of as weak though well-meaning persons and crotchety folks, as Noah doubtless was considered by *his* friends.

The ancient Roman proverb says, 'Whom God means to destroy, He first deprives of reason,' and if this proverb was ever applicable, it is so to nominal Christians who thus proclaim their ignorance and madness by destroying the food sent to them by God for the support of the people.

What would the world say, if every baker in Britain, instead of going his round to replenish each empty bread-store, was to proceed, say on next Monday morning, to pile up all his bread in a heap at his door, mixed with combustible materials, and, setting the whole on fire, consume it to ashes? Or, if each farmer, as soon as he had secured his crop in the corn-yard, was to set fire to it and utterly destroy the whole?

When the newspapers report that a stack of corn has been burnt by some ill-disposed criminal, the whole country is alarmed, and bloodhounds are got to track the villain to his guilty den, in order to his being severely punished. Yet, in truth, the mad-like baker, farmer, and incendiary, would be wise, compared with those who deliberately convert grain into malt liquor and spirits ; for the bread or grain burners would merely add somewhat to the hunger, or sickness, or deaths around us from *want* of food ; while the brewer, distiller, and their supporters, besides inducing hunger, sickness, and death, are the chief promoters of nearly all the crime and misery in our land. This is no imaginary accusation, but a plain undeniable fact, acknowledged by every person connected with the investigation of crime and punishment.

In the 11th chapter of Proverbs, v. 26, we read, 'He that *withholdeth* grain, the people SHALL curse him.' Solomon, inspired with wisdom from God, declares that those who '*withheld*' corn—of course merely that it might rise to a famine price—should be detested and *cursed*. Any one can imagine how he would have designated persons who *burnt their grain* in presence of an underfed or starving people. Yet it is clearly a greater crime to destroy God-given food, by converting it into what maddens myriads into criminals, than merely to burn it.

How can a consistent Christian condemn suicide, and at the same time deliberately act so as to injure his own health, and thus shorten his life? The poor insane victim of suicide generally has his mind unhinged by some real or imaginary calamity; while the moderate, alcohol-drinking Christian damages his health, and thus shortens his life, either to gratify a contemptible lust of the flesh, or to avoid giving offence to the world.

It is easy to see which of these two God will judge most severely. Will His wrath be disarmed by the alcohol drinker's having 'only shortened his life a little'? Who gave him liberty to do this? What right have we to diminish by one day the time appointed by God for our serving Him on earth? Will the plea of ignorance as to the injurious effect of alcohol on their souls and bodies, be accepted from those who have this truth daily and plainly set before them, and illustrated in the fearful amount of crime and misery confessedly springing up all

c

around us from alcohol? or because some medical man advised them to use it *as a medicine* when sick, and they chose, when in health, to continue its use?

'God will not be mocked,' although He bear long with us; and the day is hastening on when every one will have to give in their account before Him: woe then to those who shall have no better excuse for having thus actively aided in the growth of every kind of sin, crime, and human misery, than their love of alcohol, or its base gains; who fearing the laugh of fools more than the wrath of God, turn a deaf ear to the remonstrances of those who continually warn them as to the fearful consequences of their sin.

The Apostle Paul declared, that if his eating meat made his brother to offend, he would eat no meat while the world endured, lest he should thus injure his brother. Yet we find Christians (at least persons calling themselves so) admitting that the making and drinking of alcohol is beyond dispute the daily cause of temporal and spiritual *death* to thousands, who nevertheless continue their lucrative trade, and cling to their selfish enjoyments. Such persons surely forget the warning of the Apostle James (chap. iv. 17), that 'To him who knoweth to do good and doeth it not, to him it is sin;' for all must admit that it is 'good' and right to apply the food sent from God to its proper purpose, and that it is *not* good, but sinful, to get gain by converting it into a soul and body destroying poison. If 'for every *idle word* that we speak, we shall have to give account,' can a Christian believe that God will welcome to Heaven those who prefer gratifying mere lusts, and complying with foolish customs, to doing the will of their Heavenly Father?

What would St Paul have said, had he, seeing the ruin and misery everywhere caused by the making and drinking of intoxicating liquor in the present day, been invited to give up his trade of a tent-maker to become a wine-maker, a brewer, a distiller, a keeper of a dram-shop, or an encourager in any imaginable way of such polluting traffic?

The Christian conscience will instantly find the indignant reply, 'Is thy servant a dog, that he should do this thing?' and add, that if *St Paul* needed continually to 'press on for the prize of his high calling in Christ Jesus,' those who in comparison with him are merely dreaming about Christianity, ought to shrink far more carefully from contact with anything that leads to temptation, to danger of separation from God and to eternal death; whether on their own account, or for those brethren around them whose keeper God certainly expects us to be.

Such are some of the reasons why a Christian, if in health, should refuse to drink intoxicating liquors of every description; and science is daily making it more and more clear, that even giving it as a remedy in disease, is often a serious and fatal error.

Those who prefer gratifying the sinful lusts of the flesh, although at the cost of injuring their health, slightly or seriously, according to the quantity drank, will probably continue thus to offend God and induce others to do the same: but earnest Christians, who love and desire to please God, will ponder all these things carefully, and pray that He may give them grace to ABSTAIN.

APPENDIX ON WINES.

—

The *Lancet* has just completed a short series of reports upon the red wines of France, the clarets and the Burgundies, and the red wines of Hungary and Greece. It appears from the analyses that the mean strength in alcohol of all the clarets examined was 9 grains per cent.; of the Burgundies 9⅓ grains—that is, the latter were very little stronger than the former. The mean alcoholic strength of the Hungarian wines was just 10 grains per cent.; while the mean strength of the two Greek wines was 11 grains per cent. Some of the clarets and Burgundies analysed contained *added spirit and sugar.* There was no relation between the *quantities of spirit* contained in the several wines and the *price*, some of the cheaper containing more spirit than the dearer. Some time since Baron Liebig promulgated the statement that Hungarian wines contained a larger amount of phosphoric acid than most other wines; and to this circumstance a superiority was attributed! The analyses now published afford no support to that assertion, as the mean amount was found to be about the same as in the clarets, but less than in the Burgundies. It is a common belief that wine possesses highly nourishing properties. In order to form an exact opinion on this point, the nitrogen present in each of the wines tested was determined, and the mean amount of albuminous matter in 1,000 grain measures of the wines was found to be only 1⅓ grain; while in 1,000 grains' weight of lean beef it was 207 grains—that is to say, the raw flesh of beef contains 156 times more nourishment than wine. Consequently, the amount of nutriment contained in wine, as contrasted with meat and most articles of diet, is insignificant and infinitesimal.

New Works and Editions.

THE BIBLE COMMENTARY AND ABSTAINER'S SCRIPTURE TEXT-BOOK, containing Version, Criticism, and Exposition on every passage relating to the Temperance Question. Edited by Dr LEES and Rev D. BURNS. Price 6s. 'This is, in fact, a Bible of Temperance.'

KALON OINON: OR, THE MIRACLE AT CANA; AND PRIZE ESSAY ON DEUTERONOMY xiv. 26 (mistranslated strong drink). Price 3d., or 12 copies for 2s.

> 'Dr LEES' works are full of truth.'—*Archdeacon Sandford.*

> 'No writer,' says Professor DOUGLAS, M.D., 'has devoted so much time and research to the subject as Dr LEES. His principal positions have never been successfully assailed. Without following him implicitly, we agree with him in the main.'— Article 'Wine,' in Principal FAIRBAIRN's *Imperial Bible Dictionary* (1867).

DOCTORS, DRUGS, AND DRINK; or, IS ALCOHOL A MEDICINE? By Dr LEES. Paper, 10d.; Cloth, 1s. 4d.

TEN LECTURES ON TEMPERANCE. By Dr E. NOTT. Students' Edition, 6s.; People's Edition, 1s.; Cloth, 1s. 4d.

WORKS OF DR LEES.—Vol. I., on the Moral, Social, Religious, Chemical, and Medical Aspects of the Temperance Question, 5s. Vol. II., on the Historical and Biblical, 7s. Vol. III., on the Zoo-Chemistry and Physiology of Teetotalism, 5s. Vol. IV. being Prize Essay on Prohibition and Sequels, 3s. 6d.

BRUSSELS CONGRESS ADDRESS, with Map of Crime, paged to bind up with the £100 ALLIANCE PRIZE ESSAY, 5d.

LAW AND LIBERTY, in reply to J. S. MILL and others, 3d.

IS ALCOHOL FOOD ? An exposure of the *Manchester Examiner's* Attack on Teetotalism, with an able Article by Professor PEASELEY, in reply to the *Westminster*, 3*d*.

STANDARD TEMPERANCE DOCUMENTS : containing Valuable Reprints from Medical Authors of the last two centuries, and a mass of evidence on the Wines of the Ancients, 2*s*.

THE BIBLE A TEMPERANCE BOOK. New Edition, 3*d*. ; with NEW TESTAMENT LECTURE added, 5*d*.

LETTER TO A CURATE : being an Exposition and Defence of New Testament Temperance, with much new Information on difficult Texts, 3*d*.

A VINDICATION OF THE BIBLE, TEETOTAL-ISM, and DR LEES, from the Fallacies of the Rev D. WILLIAMS' 2*s*. BOOK OF BLUNDERS, 4*d*.

'Dr LEES is an ingenious and inexhaustible writer; skilled in the science and practice of logic.'—*Manchester Examiner*.

APOSTOLIC NEEPHALISM : a critique on the Dean of Down's famous Letter. 3 copies for 6*d*.

EPIDEMIC WHIMS ; or, Teetotalism and Prohibition, in reply to ISAAC TAYLOR's chapter in 'Ultimate Civilisation,' 2*d*.

SACRAMENTAL WINE QUESTION : being the First Prize Essay ; and Answers to the Rev Dr HALLEY's Objections, 6*d*. ; abridged, 2*d*.

THE TRUTH-SEEKER : an Organ of Philosophical Discussion. First Series: 3 vols., 7*s*. ; Second Series : 2 large octavo vols., 5*s*.

ILLUSTRATED HISTORY OF ALCOHOL : with Sewall's Small Plates of the Stomach, coloured, 5*s*.

COLOSSAL DRAWINGS of the Stomach. Liver, Kidneys, and Brain. in 9 large sheets, illustrating the ravages of Alcohol, 20*s*.

THE INNER HISTORY OF THE TEMPERANCE
LIBEL CASE FROM THE MORAL STAND-POINT:
being Final Words. Parts I. and II., 1s.

'Part I. is as dramatic and interesting as a novel.' Part
II. 'A more extraordinary publication we have seldom read.
If generally circulated, it would change public opinion, and
astonish not a few by its revelations.'—*Newcastle Chronicle.*

REFUTATION OF THE WESTMINSTER RE-
VIEWER (70 pages), 1s.

'A masterly and merciless exposure.'—*Alliance News.*

'Sweeps away his logic with resistless force.'—*Christian
News.*

'Those who delight in philosophical polemics, will have a
rich treat in this masterly refutation.'—*Boston Guardian.*

TESTIMONIAL REPORT, with the Speeches, on the
presentation of 1,000 Guineas to Dr LEES, in the Leeds Town
Hall, 3d.

REV. W. COOKE'S FOSSIL OBJECTIONS, Disen-
tombed from his old Pamphlet, 'Teetotalism Purified.' 4d.
per dozen.

FALLACIES OF DR INMAN AND OF DR
ANSTIE in the 'CORNHILL MAGAZINE.' 3d.

A CHAPTER OF TEMPERANCE HISTORY:
being an account of the Diplomacy which led to the *Inter-
national Temperance and Prohibition Convention* of 1862.
Printed so as to bind up with the published volume of its
proceedings. 2d.

THE TEETOTAL TOPIC: 60 quarto pages, 6d.

[1d. per 1s. to be added for postage.]

Post-free from DR F. R. LEES, Meanwood Lodge, Leeds.

BECKETT BROTHERS, PRINTERS, OSSETT.

ERRATA.

The reader will please correct the following
printer's errors:—

Page 16, *line* 6 from bottom,—strike out *al* and *w* in
'allowed,' making the word into 'loved.'

Page 27, *line* 6 from bottom,—change *a* in 'mea' into
ri, so as to read 'meri.'